Growing Through Arts

by *Aleksandra* ℠

THE
Cinderella
BALLET

BY *Aleksandra* SM

BALLET SERIES

Growing Through Arts

ORCHID PUBLISHING | CHICAGO

    Director of Publications
    Orchid Publishing, Inc.
    333 N. Michigan Ave., #222
    Chicago, IL 60601
    www.orchid-publishing.com

Illustrations by Elizaveta Efimova

Special Thanks to Russian Pointe Dance Boutique, Joffrey Ballet, Scott Speck, Auditorium Theatre of Roosevelt
University, River North Dance Company and Vala Dancewear for Glossary photos.

Library of Congress Control Number: 2010918290
ISBN 978-0-9831641-1-1

Production Date: January 20, 2011
Printing Plant Location: Everbest Printing Co. Ltd.,
   Nansha, China
Job/Batch #: EPC-RN-97951.4 R4

The story of *Cinderella* is a timeless classic, told and retold in various languages, role-played by countless little girls who imagine themselves to be Cinderella, rising above "impossible" odds to dance at the ball with the Prince.

Cinderella has also inspired audiences on ballet stages around the world. Before Prokofiev wrote his famous score, the story had already been set to dance many, many times. It is a tale perfectly paired with the art of ballet.

Ballet can have a powerful and uplifting effect. Besides the impact of the performance itself—the masterful dancers, the spectacular sets, the thrill of the live orchestra—it can impart valuable life lessons that stay with us for a lifetime.

One of the amazing things about *Cinderella* is its adaptability. Not only has this story been embraced by cultures around the world, but it has also been reinterpreted, over and over, for changing times and values. Our version of the story contains all of the familiar and well-loved story elements but also accentuates Cinderella's passion for dance and her *focused desire* to achieve her dreams. We think it's an inspiring interpretation that will resonate with both children and parents today.

Welcome to the enchanting story of Cinderella. May all of your child's dreams, like Cinderella's, come true—in dance and in every part of life!

Ever Growing Through Arts,
Aleksandra

How to Use This Book.

🖎 Read the story to your child many times to encourage memory and to explore the themes more deeply.

🖎 Pretend you're in a theater, watching the "ballet" unfold on stage!

🖎 Read and discuss Miss Aleksandra's Themes & Values, integrated throughout the book, and look for ways to relate them to your child's life.

🖎 At the end of the book, use Miss Aleksandra's Glossary to learn the new vocabulary words introduced in the story and to enjoy beautiful photo illustrations of ballet concepts.

🖎 Engage in a thoughtful dialogue with your child—ask questions about the story, pictures, and characters.

🖎 Expand your fun and learning time with your child by doing activities in the Practice & Play book (sold separately), which integrates characters and story elements from the storybook.

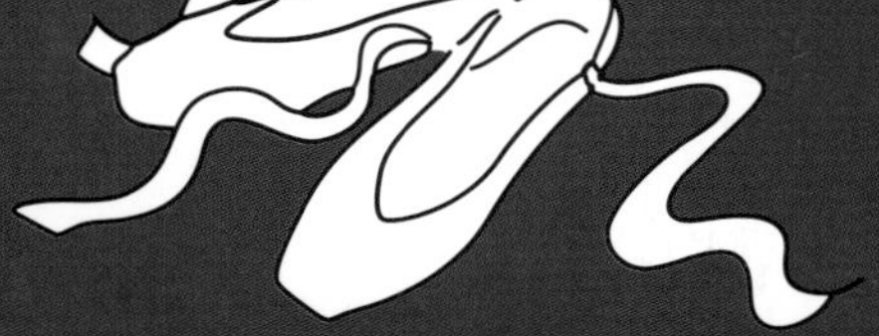

Welcome to the theater!

Tonight's performance will be *Cinderella*, by Sergei Prokofiev. **Backstage** the dancers **warm up** as the **musicians** tune their instruments. The audience waits excitedly for the ballet to begin. The curtain opens! Now the dancers begin to tell their tale . . .

Once upon a time, a girl named Cinderella lived with her stepfamily. Cinderella dreamed of being a dancer. But her stepmother didn't care about Cinderella's dreams. She cared only about Cinderella's *chores*.

It was Cinderella's job to scrub floors, wash dishes, and tend to the fire, while her stepsisters drank tea, brushed their hair, and chattered about marrying princes. "Work harder, Cinderella!" they would say.

8

Do you think it's important to have dreams and goals? Why?

Cinderella never complained. Doing chores gave her a chance to **rehearse** her dance steps and dream her dreams. "Sweeping is my *favorite* job," she would tell her friends, the kitchen mice. Cinderella loved to pretend she was a **ballerina** and the broom was a **male dancer**. She would swirl and spin about the kitchen floor, making believe it was a grand ballroom.

Cinderella has a positive attitude. She makes the best of a bad situation by using it to help her achieve her dreams. Are there some ways you can do this?

At night, while her stepfamily slept, she would practice the ballet exercises her real mother had taught her and read books by the fire's embers.

It's important to dream, but it's also important to study and practice. Dreams and practice together are an unbeatable combination!

Cinderella was as kind as she was graceful and studious. One morning an old woman appeared at the kitchen window, asking for food. Her stepsisters shouted, "Go away, hag! No food here!" But Cinderella slipped her own breakfast into her pocket and snuck outside.

"Please," she told the old woman, "take this. And may your luck change for the better!"

"May yours too," said the woman with a wink.

MISS *Aleksandra's* THEMES & VALUES

Kindness often has surprising rewards. Have you ever been kind to anyone? Has anyone ever been kind to you? How did you feel?

Later that day, a letter arrived from the palace! Cinderella's stepsisters were bursting with excitement but didn't know how to read. "What does it say?" they asked Cinderella. "The Prince is hosting a Ball!" announced Cinderella, reading the note. "Tonight, at the palace. And *we* are invited!"

"Not *you*, Cinderella," laughed her stepsisters. "Just us." And they hurried off to buy things for the ball, leaving Cinderella behind.

MISS *Aleksandra's* THEMES & VALUES

Cinderella is a great reader. That means she can learn things her stepsisters can't!
Is it nice for Cinderella's stepsisters to leave her out of their plans?

Cinderella sighed. "Someday *I'll* wear a beautiful gown and dance at a ball."
She owned only one tattered house-dress that she wore every day.

"Cheer up, Cinderella," said her mouse friends. "We'll have our own ball!"

The mice scurried about the house, gathering scraps of cloth. Cinderella's bird friends
stitched them together into a "gown." It wasn't much to look at but Cinderella said,
"It's the most beautiful gown I've ever seen," and put it on.

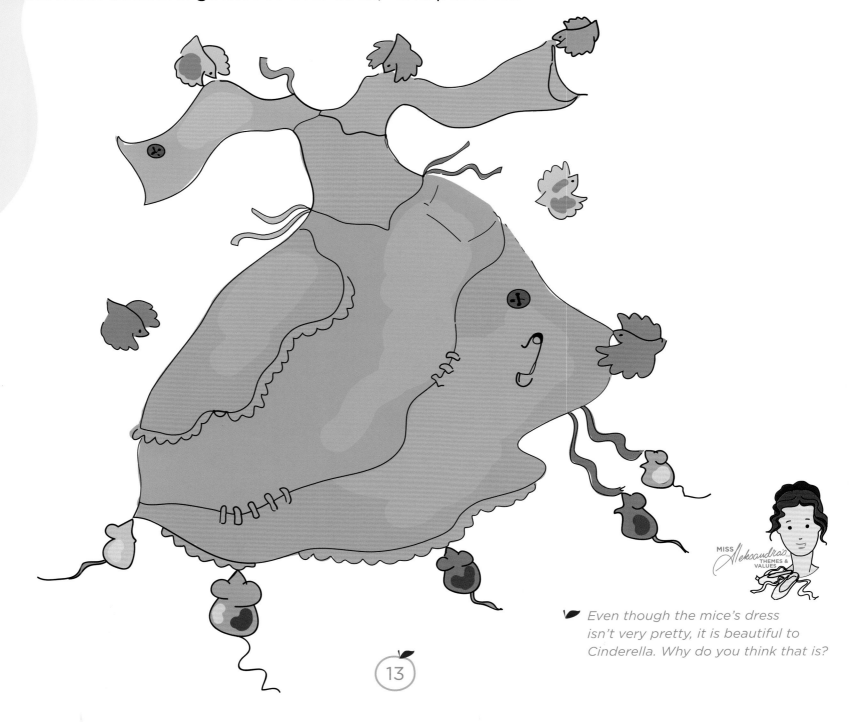

Even though the mice's dress isn't very pretty, it is beautiful to Cinderella. Why do you think that is?

"Dance for us, Cinderella!" cheered the mice. "Oh, please!" Cinderella put
on the **pointe shoes** her mother had given her and began to dance a **solo**.
Soon she was swept away by her imagination.
In her mind she saw magical fairies
dancing! They made *her* want to
dance even more beautifully.

*When you see someone else doing
something beautifully, does it inspire
you to perform better yourself?*

When she opened her eyes, something strange had happened. She was wearing the same gown she'd worn in her imagination! Standing before her was a real, live fairy, glowing with light from inside.

"I know you!" gasped Cinderella. "You're the woman who came to our window!"

"Yes, but I'm *really* your Fairy Godmother," said the fairy. "And tonight all your kindness and hard work will be rewarded. *You* shall go to the Prince's Ball. And you shall look and feel like the princess you already are inside."

The fairy godmother knows that Cinderella is already beautiful on the inside. Beauty happens inside first, outside second.

With a sweep of her magic wand, the fairy turned the mice into great white horses and a garden pumpkin into a glorious golden carriage.

"But there is one thing you must remember, Cinderella. My magic ends at twelve o'clock! Leave the Ball before midnight!" The Fairy Godmother waved her wand again and a sparkling pair of crystal slippers appeared on Cinderella's feet. Away flew the carriage, over the treetops . . .

*The lights go down and Act 1 ends. The audience bursts into **applause**! Soon the **conductor** waves his **baton** and the orchestra starts again. It's time for Act 2 . . .*

The palace ballroom was bustling with women from all over the kingdom, eager for a chance to dance with the Prince. When it was the stepsisters' turn, the Prince danced with each of them quickly, hardly looking at their faces.

"The Prince doesn't seem to be enjoying himself," said the King.

"That's because none of the ladies can dance as well as he," said the Queen.

Just then a hush fell across the room. Cinderella stepped into the ballroom at the top of the stairs. She seemed to glow with her own inner light.

When we're feeling confident and beautiful inside, we seem to shine on the outside!

17

The Prince looked at her and felt his heart leap. As Cinderella came down the stairs **on pointe**, he fell under the spell of her beauty. He took her hand and whirled her onto the dance floor.

Cinderella and the Prince danced a **pas de deux** across the ballroom, dipping and turning together like two birds in a flock. The other dancers formed a **corps de ballet** around them. As the guests looked on, goose bumps popped on their skin.

MISS *Aleksandra's*
THEMES & VALUES

The beauty of dance can move people in special ways. Art can be very powerful.

The Prince and Cinderella danced thrilling **combinations**, gazing into each other's eyes. They forgot all about the other guests. They forgot about the King and Queen. They forgot about the floor and the four walls . . .

They even forgot about . . . the clock.

Suddenly the great palace chimes struck midnight. GONG!

MISS *Aleksandra's*
THEMES &
VALUES

Did you ever notice that when you're doing something you love, you forget about time? Why do think that is?

Cinderella remembered the fairy's warning. "Oh no!" she cried, "I must go!" She turned to run up the stairs. Too late! Leaving one crystal slipper behind, she began to change back into everyday Cinderella.

"Come back!" shouted the Prince, holding the slipper. "I love you!" But Cinderella was gone.

The next day, the Prince vowed,
"I will travel every inch of this
kingdom and find the foot
that fits the slipper."

The Prince traveled from door to door, asking every
girl in the kingdom to try on the slipper. No foot would
fit. At last there was only one house left to visit.

When Cinderella's stepmother saw the Prince
approaching her home, she said, "Go hide in your room,
Cinderella. And stay quiet!"

The Prince tried the slipper on Cinderella's
stepsisters, then her stepmother. No luck.
"Well," announced the Prince with a sigh,
"it seems there are no other ladies in
this house. Or this kingdom."

"Wait, there's me!" shouted a voice from Cinderella's room.

The Prince asked to see the hiding girl. "Surely you don't think this *cinder*-thing could be the dancer from the ball," laughed the stepmother.

It's important to obey your parents, but it's also important to speak up if you are being treated unfairly.

But when the Prince gazed into Cinderella's eyes his heart knew the truth. He placed the slipper on her foot and it fit like an acorn into its shell.

The Prince took Cinderella's hand and they danced out the door and into the square. Everyone stopped and watched, their spirits lifted by the dazzling dance.

"I think the Prince has found his bride," said the King.

"I think the Prince has found his partner," said the Queen.

"I think Cinderella has found her dream," sighed the mice.

The lights go down and the curtain closes.
The dancers take a **curtain call** as the audience
claps and cheers.
Everyone in the theater—the dancers
and the audience—
feels lighter and brighter inside.
That's the magic of ballet!

MISS *Aleksandra's* THEMES & VALUES

Cinderella and her prince find love for each other through their love for dance. Perhaps a "fairytale marriage" is about two people sharing their life as equal partners!

27

MISS *Aleksandra's*sm GLOSSARY

COURTESY RUSSIAN POINTE DANCE BOUTIQUE

backstage

COURTESY RUSSIAN POINTE DANCE BOUTIQUE

ballerina

Applause is the clapping of an audience after a performance.

"**Backstage**" means the area where dancers get ready to perform on stage. The audience cannot see backstage.

A **baton** is a thin stick that the conductor of the orchestra holds.

A female ballet dancer is called a **ballerina**.

In ballet, a **combination** is a series of dance moves strung together, one after another. Combinations create the choreography.

The **conductor** leads the orchestra, using a baton.

The **corps de ballet** is a group of dancers that perform together, not as soloists.

Dancers take a bow, or **curtain call**, when the audience applauds at the end of a performance.

Male dancer is the term for a boy or man who dances in a ballet.

conductor

curtain call

male dancer

musicians

pas de deux

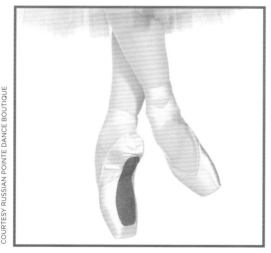

pointe shoes

Musicians are the artists who play musical instruments in the orchestra.

To dance **on pointe** (or en pointe) means to dance on the tips of the toes.

A **pas de deux** in ballet is a dance that two dancers perform together.

Pointe shoes are special shoes worn by ballerinas that allow them to dance on the tips of their toes. This takes a lot of training and practice!

Dancers must practice, or **rehearse**, their dance steps over and over in order to learn them.

A **solo** is a dance performed by one person.

Dancers do **warm-up** exercises before a performance to get their muscles ready to dance.

rehearse

solo

warm-up

ABOUT
Aleksandra [SM]

Aleksandra Efimova is the founder of **Growing Through Arts**™ and President of Russian Pointe, Inc., a brand of luxury ballet shoes with a flagship boutique on Chicago's Magnificent Mile. Born in St. Petersburg, Russia, Aleksandra graduated from the renowned Art School at the Hermitage State Art Museum and received training in classical dance, art, and academics. In 1993, she moved to United States, where she started her first successful company while still an undergraduate student. An alumna of Harvard Business School, she is an inspirational speaker and writer and is actively involved in promoting the arts, international collaboration, and education in the community.

OTHER BOOKS IN
THE GROWING THROUGH ARTS™

BALLET SERIES

The Nutcracker Ballet by Aleksandra[SM] (storybook)

The Sleeping Beauty Ballet by Aleksandra[SM] (storybook)

The Nutcracker Ballet Practice & Play Book by Aleksandra[SM]

The Cinderella Ballet Practice & Play Book by Aleksandra[SM]

The Sleeping Beauty Ballet Practice & Play Book by Aleksandra[SM]

MUSIC SERIES

The Peter and the Wolf Symphony by Aleksandra[SM] (storybook)

The Snow Maiden Opera by Aleksandra[SM] (storybook)

Twist, A Musical by Aleksandra[SM] (storybook)

The Peter and the Wolf Symphony Practice & Play Book by Aleksandra[SM]

The Snow Maiden Opera Practice & Play Book by Aleksandra[SM]

Twist, A Musical Practice & Play Book by Aleksandra[SM]

rough Ar

ugh

Gro

Growing Thro